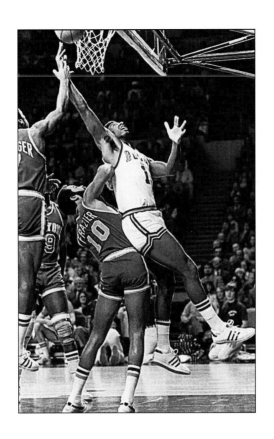

Milwaukee Bucks

Jack C. Harris

Published by Creative Education
123 South Broad Street, Mankato, Minnesota 56001
Creative Education is an imprint of The Creative Company

Designed by Rita Marshall

Photos by: Allsport Photography, Associated Press/Wide World Photos,
Focus on Sports, NBA Photos, UPI/Corbis-Bettmann, and SportsChrome.

Photo page 1: Oscar Robertson
Photo title page: Johnny Newman

Library of Congress Cataloging-in-Publication Data

Harris, Jack C.
Milwaukee Bucks / Jack C. Harris.
p. cm. — (NBA today)
Summary: Highlights the players, coaches, playing strategies, and
memorable games in the history of the Milwaukee Bucks basketball team.
ISBN 0-88682-880-5

1. Milwaukee Bucks (Basketball team)—Juvenile literature.
[1. Milwaukee Bucks (Basketball team)—History. 2. Basketball—History.]
I. Title. II. Series: NBA today (Mankato, Minn.)

GV885.52.M54H37 1997   96-51059
796.323'64'0977595—dc21

First edition

5 4 3 2 1

The state of Wisconsin has a heritage built upon several different cultures. In the early 1600s, the area was explored by French traders and then settled by people of French and German backgrounds. Both French and British governors ruled the area before it finally became part of the United States. But before the Europeans created this rich history, the territory was home to numerous noble Native American nations. That's why the map of Wisconsin is peppered with such town names as Baraboo, Menomonie, Oshkosh, and Weyauwega.

The largest and best known of all of Wisconsin's Native

NBA legend Kareem Abdul-Jabbar.

Future Hall of Famer Guy Rodgers was featured on the Bucks' first roster.

American named cities is Milwaukee. Its fame is based on its importance as a port on Lake Michigan and as the beer-making center of America. But for sports fans throughout the Midwest, Milwaukee is famous as the home of one of the most successful National Basketball Association (NBA) franchises of the past 30 years—the Milwaukee Bucks.

While the names of some of Wisconsin's cities might be hard to remember or pronounce, a basketball fan easily recalls the names and exploits of some of the great athletes who have starred for the Milwaukee Bucks in the past—such outstanding players as Quinn Buckner, Bobby Dandridge, Bob Lanier, Marques Johnson, Sidney Moncrief, Jack Sikma, and the legendary Oscar Robertson and Kareem Abdul-Jabbar. And such Bucks players as Ray Allen, Vin Baker, and Glenn Robinson are today establishing names for themselves among basketball fans in Milwaukee and throughout the country.

THE NBA LEAVES AND RETURNS TO MILWAUKEE

While the Bucks have nearly always had strong support, Milwaukee was not always known as a great pro basketball city. Older fans and sports historians remember the day back in 1955 when the old Milwaukee Hawks were forced to move to St. Louis, Missouri. Why did the Hawks have to leave? At the time, NBA president Maurice Podoloff was quoted as saying, "If Milwaukee fans won't support their team, we have no choice but to find a city that will."

Milwaukee was without an NBA franchise for more than a decade. Then, early in 1968, it was decided that the NBA would give Wisconsin fans a second chance. League officials

"The Big O," Oscar Robertson.

announced that two new teams would join the league for the 1968–69 season—the Suns in Phoenix, Arizona, and the Bucks in Milwaukee.

After arriving in a trade with Chicago, Flynn Robinson quickly became the Bucks' top scorer.

Milwaukee fans were excited to have a new team to support, but they were also aware that the new squad was bound to have some growing pains. As an expansion team, the Bucks would have to build their roster with castoffs from the older NBA clubs and inexperienced rookies chosen through the college draft. It would be the job of the team's first coach—Larry Costello, a former NBA player and assistant coach—to mold these players into a competitive unit. Costello's first Bucks lineup included such relative unknowns or aging veterans as forwards Lenny Chappell, Don Smith, and Greg Smith; guards Jon McGlocklin, Guy Rodgers, and Flynn Robinson; and center Wayne Embry, the team's "big man," who stood only 6-foot-8.

Not surprisingly, the 1968–69 season ended with the Bucks in the division cellar with a mere 27 wins. The most impressive thing about the rookie Bucks was their home attendance record. These raw players, on a new team, were cheered by more home fans than any other expansion team in NBA history. Milwaukee fans proved that they could indeed support an NBA franchise.

A COIN TOSS CHANGES BUCKS HISTORY

The Bucks' last-place finish in 1968–69 had a silver lining. According to the draft rules of the NBA, the team with the poorest record in each division could participate in a coin toss to decide which would be allowed to choose first in the annual college draft. Lowest in the East, the Bucks flipped a coin with Western cellar dweller, Phoenix, and won the right to choose one of the best players in college history—7-foot-2 Lew Alcindor, who had played center for UCLA. During his three years with the Bruins, UCLA lost only two games and became the first college team to win three consecutive NCAA championships.

Known today as Kareem Abdul-Jabbar, Alcindor began his pro career by signing a five-year $1.4 million contract as number 33 for Milwaukee. Local basketball fans were uneasy at first, not believing that a rookie could be worth so much cash. But Alcindor put any fears to rest during the opening seconds of his first game as a Buck. He snared the opening tip-off against the Suns and then raced toward a spot near the basket, ready to receive a pass. Alcindor smoothly outjumped a pair of Phoenix defenders for the ball and sank a perfect skyhook. At game's end, the Bucks had narrowly defeated the Suns 87–86, and Alcindor's stats read 24 points, 23 rebounds, and 11 blocked shots. It was the start of an exciting NBA career.

After the game, all anyone could talk about was Alcindor's performance. "He's the best man I've ever seen," said Bucks teammate Guy Rodgers, who had played part of his career with the legendary Wilt Chamberlain. Even the losing coach, Phoenix's Johnny Kerr, had to say, "Alcindor's going to put a lot of people into retirement."

Alcindor's fine play as a rookie inspired the other Bucks as well. In only its second season, Milwaukee burned up the NBA courts with a dazzling 56–26 record, which put it solidly in second place in the NBA's Eastern Division. That

1 9 7 0

Bobby Dandridge joined Lew Alcindor on the NBA's All-Rookie team.

Big shooters in the middle, Bobby Dandridge . . .

. . . and Bob Lanier.

was quite a change from the club's last-place finish the year before. Not only was Alcindor the hands-down choice for the NBA Rookie of the Year in 1969–70, but teammates Bobby Dandridge, Jon McGlocklin, Flynn Robinson, and Greg Smith all achieved the best records of their careers that season as well.

1 9 7 1

An accurate outside shooter, Jon McGlocklin sank nearly 54 percent of his field goal tries.

THE "BIG O" EARNS HIS CHAMPIONSHIP RING

The Bucks' rapid turnaround during 1969–70 inspired team management to believe the club could soon win an NBA championship. All that was needed, they felt, was an experienced leader and playmaker to run the team's offense. With most Milwaukee fans in agreement, the Bucks traded Charlie Paulk and Flynn Robinson to the Cincinnati Royals for the "Big O," Oscar Robertson.

Robertson, now in basketball's Hall of Fame, was a spectacular guard who performed flawlessly on the court. He was a great shooter, ball handler, and rebounder. Even more impressive was Robertson's ability to outthink his opponents. Playing in Cincinnati, Robertson had already earned an NBA Most Valuable Player trophy as well as a trio of All-Star Game MVP awards before he arrived in Milwaukee. A championship ring was the one thing the "Big O" had never garnered. Now, teamed with Alcindor and the other young Bucks stars, Robertson's ring seemed a real possibility. Yet the "Big O" was careful not to put the ring's importance in the forefront. "The championship isn't what I've been waiting for all these years," he stated. "If it comes, it comes."

Robertson's teammates knew how their new leader really

felt, however, and they were eager to help him. "Oscar wants that championship badly," said Lew Alcindor. "Me, I've got time. But Oscar wants it right now, and he's got us all feeling that way."

Even if Robertson downplayed his desire to own a championship ring in the press, out on the court he looked as if he was driving as hard as he could for it. Aided in the back court by Jon McGlocklin and Lucius Allen, the "Big O" directed the third-year club to a league-best 66–16 record. The spectacular 1970–71 season included an NBA record 20-game winning streak. Robertson also helped Alcindor become an even better player. The big center ended his second year in Milwaukee with a 31.9 scoring average, tops in the NBA, and the first of his six league MVP awards.

1 9 7 2

Kareem Abdul-Jabbar won his second (and last) NBA scoring title in his fourth year in the league.

With the regular season over, the Bucks began concentrating on the playoffs. Milwaukee first breezed past the San Francisco Warriors and then the Los Angeles Lakers to earn a spot in the NBA finals against the Baltimore Bullets. The Bucks pounded Baltimore in the first two games of the series, then fought a close battle in game three before escaping with a 107–99 win. Two nights later, Milwaukee completed a four-game sweep of the Bullets for the NBA title. After 11 long years and 866 games, Oscar Robertson had finally earned his NBA championship ring.

The Bucks came close to winning a second NBA crown three years later. Led by Kareem Abdul-Jabbar (the name Lew Alcindor chose for himself when he converted to the Muslim faith), Oscar Robertson, and silky-smooth forward Bobby Dandridge, Milwaukee won its fourth straight Midwest Division title in 1973–74. The Bucks then crushed the

13

Los Angeles Lakers and Chicago Bulls to reach the NBA finals against the Boston Celtics.

The Celtics-Bucks series was filled with drama. After the first five games, Boston held a three-games-to-two edge. Galloping into Boston Garden, the Celtics fully expected to wipe out the Bucks in game six. But Jabbar would not let his team go down easily, and the game went into double overtime. With Boston holding a slim 102–101 lead and only three seconds remaining, Jabbar, ignoring the wild cheering of the Boston fans, sank one of his famous skyhooks to win the game for the Bucks and force a seventh and deciding contest in Milwaukee.

To the dismay of their hometown fans, the Bucks had a sudden attack of wild shooting in that seventh game against Boston and were unable to score at all during the game's last five minutes. The final score was Celtics 102, Bucks 87. The Celts returned to Boston with their 12th NBA title in 18 years. The Bucks, meanwhile, began a rapid decline.

1 9 7 3

Lucius Allen combined with Oscar Robertson to hand out nearly 1,000 assists during the season.

MAKING CHANGES IN MILWAUKEE

Personnel changes and injuries contributed to the Bucks' fall from the top ranks of the NBA following the 1973–74 season. The first change occurred when Oscar Robertson announced his retirement. In his honor, Robertson's number 1 became the Buck's first retired jersey. It was hung from the rafters high above the Milwaukee Arena floor for fans to see and remember forever.

A second setback for the team was the decision to trade Lucius Allen, the Bucks' high-scoring starting guard, to the

14   *The sensational Kareem Abdul-Jabbar.*

Noted for his quick hands, point guard Jim Price recorded 111 steals in only 50 games.

Los Angeles Lakers for Jim Price. Price was expected to replace Oscar Robertson as point guard and also provide some of the scoring punch that Allen had given the team. Price worked hard, but he just didn't blend with the other Bucks the way Allen had.

A third factor in the Bucks' decline was an injury to the team's leader. During a preseason exhibition game, Jabbar leaped for a loose ball. Coming too close to an opponent's outstretched hand, Jabbar was jabbed in the eye. In a fit of pain, he swung his fist into a backboard post with all his might. He came away with an injured eye and a broken hand.

When Jabbar returned after missing nearly 20 games, he was sporting a large pair of protective yellow goggles. Perhaps it was his hand injury or his sore eye or his new eye gear—or a combination of all three—that made Jabbar play a bit below par for the rest of the 1974–75 season. He explained it by saying, "I'm down to my last pair of eyeballs."

Just as they were initially inspired by him, the Bucks seemed to follow Jabbar even during a slump. At season's end, they found themselves in the basement of their division with a 38–44 record. It was only the second losing season in the club's brief history.

Rumors began to circulate that Jabbar wanted to return to Los Angeles to play basketball. There was even talk about his being dissatisfied with coach Larry Costello's handling of the Bucks. Most Milwaukee fans just brushed these rumors aside. They couldn't envision their team without Kareem Abdul-Jabbar.

But then, on June 16, 1975, the announcement of a big

trade was indeed made: Kareem Abdul-Jabbar and reserve center Walt Wesley were sent to the Los Angeles Lakers in return for Lakers center Elmore Smith, guard Brian Winters, and two top draft picks, David Meyers and Junior Bridgeman. Many Bucks fans called that day "Dark Monday." Bucks general manager Wayne Embry explained why his club had traded its finest player ever. "We regret seeing Kareem go, but we had to be realistic. When a situation like this [a team's decline] happens, you do it," he said.

In his first year with the Bucks, Elmore Smith averaged 11.4 rebounds a game.

What the Bucks had done was acquire several young potential stars. The trade was the beginning of a youth movement in Milwaukee, a trend that would eventually prompt sportswriters to call the next few seasons the Bucks' "green and growing years."

It was going to take awhile for the Bucks to see success once more. Anxious Milwaukee fans suffered through two more sorry seasons. In November 1976, the frustration showed on coach Costello's face as he stepped down, turning over his duties to his assistant, Don Nelson. "I just think it's the best decision for everyone concerned," said Costello.

Costello's announcement stunned Nelson. "I'm still in shock," he told reporters. "Truthfully, I can't tell you that I'm ready for the job. I know I can do the job, but I want to be sure the players know I can do it. I need to earn their respect, that's important. As a coach I may not always be liked, but the respect of my players is critical."

Coach Nelson's first Bucks squad lacked experience and confidence, but it did feature the developing talents of such players as Junior Bridgeman, Quinn Buckner, Alex English,

David Meyers, and Swen Nater. With these players forming a solid base on which to build, Nelson turned his eye to the 1977 college draft. It was his first as the Bucks' head coach, and he made the most of his opportunity by selecting three outstanding rookies—Indiana center Kent Benson, University of Tennessee forward Ernie Grunfeld, and UCLA star forward Marques Johnson. Nelson was now ready to lead the Bucks back to their former glory.

1 9 7 7

Quinn Buckner set a team high with nine steals in a game vs. Indiana.

THE NELSON YEARS

Coach Nelson's "green and growing" team quickly grew up during the 1977–78 season. Led by rookie Marques Johnson, who averaged 19.5 points and 10.6 rebounds per game in his first season, the young squad literally ran its way to a 44–38 record and a return to the playoffs for the first time in four years. The Bucks got past Phoenix in the first round before being eliminated by Denver.

It was clear to Milwaukee fans that Don Nelson had set in motion a process that would bring brighter tomorrows to the Bucks. But those tomorrows were a little farther away than they realized. A career-threatening injury to star forward David Meyers and the decision of high-scoring Alex English to leave Milwaukee for free agency weakened the team. As a result, the Bucks' record fell to 38–44 in 1978–79, and the club failed to make the playoffs again.

Once again Nelson looked to the college draft for help. He set his sights on University of Arkansas All-American guard Sidney Moncrief and made him the Bucks' number one choice. This proved to be a wise decision. Moncrief's intelligence and leadership turned out to be highlights of the 1979–80 season and many years to come. One of the low points was the slow development of third-year Bucks center Kent Benson. He was always under a lot of pressure to fill the shoes of Kareem Abdul-Jabbar in Milwaukee, and Benson was never quite able to meet fans' expectations of him.

Midway through the 1979–80 season, Benson was traded to the Detroit Pistons for veteran Bob Lanier, a powerful 6-foot-11 scoring sensation who was already recognized as one of the best centers in the NBA. Lanier helped put the Bucks back on the winning track and into the playoffs. Lanier was certain that the Bucks could go all the way to a second NBA championship. "It might be destiny," he was quoted as saying. Unfortunately, the Seattle SuperSonics had different ideas, and the Sonics eliminated the Bucks, four games to three, in the first round.

It was a time of reflection for Don Nelson. As a player for the Boston Celtics, Nelson had been coached by the legendary Red Auerbach, who had guided the club to 11 world championships in 13 seasons. After being a part of this fabled team, Nelson would never be content to go down in the record books without a title shot of his own.

Nelson confessed, "I learned many things from Red. One of the most useful was how to stay hungry. The long season and constant pressure of the NBA will take some of the steam out of the players. But even more dangerous is the tendency to let down after a winning season. The great teams learn how to win night after night, week after week, season after season, with no letup."

Under Nelson's leadership, the Bucks became one of the

1 9 7 8

Long-range hitter Brian Winters led the Bucks in scoring with a 19.9 point average.

Guard Sidney Moncrief.

most consistent winners in the NBA. During the 1980s, the club racked up seven consecutive division titles and won 50 or more games seven times. One of the secrets to Nelson's success was his ability to adapt his system to the talents of each of his players. "Some coaches," said Sidney Moncrief, "are so stubborn, that if a player has a certain strength but that player doesn't exactly fit into what he wants to do, the player is lost. Nellie makes sure there are options in our offense for everybody."

Marques Johnson completed his second consecutive season as the Bucks' scoring and rebounding leader.

Bucks guard Paul Pressey added, "Nellie gets the most out of his players because he lets you get a feel for what he wants you to do by allowing you the freedom to do what you do best."

One of the players who always did his best under Nelson's system was Sidney Moncrief. For example, during the 1981–82 season, the 6-foot-4 swingman became the first player since Hall of Famer John Havlicek of the 1970 Celtics to lead his team in scoring, rebounds, assists, and minutes played in the same year. The next two seasons he was honored as the NBA's best defensive player as well.

Led by Moncrief, Lanier, and Marques Johnson—and later by Paul Pressey, Terry Cummings, and Ricky Pierce—Nelson's Bucks reached the Eastern Conference finals in 1982–83, 1983–84, and 1985–86. Yet each time they fell to either the Boston Celtics or Philadelphia 76ers and failed to reach the NBA championship round.

Before the 1986–87 season, Nelson engineered a trade he thought could finally bring Milwaukee an NBA crown. He acquired 6-foot-10 Jack Sikma, a 10-year veteran, from the Seattle SuperSonics for center Alton Lister and two first-

1 9 8 2

Sidney Moncrief's outstanding season on offense and defense put him on the All-NBA team.

round draft choices. With Sikma in the pivot, the 1986–87 Bucks had the new look Nelson was seeking. However, both Paul Pressey and Sidney Moncrief were soon lost to injuries, and the team could not live up to expectations. For the first time since the 1978–79 season, Milwaukee did not win its division championship. Still, the year was not without its bright spots. For example, Ricky Pierce and Craig Hodges began developing into outstanding players who would make their marks in seasons to come.

But the Bucks' future suddenly became uncertain. In an abrupt move, Don Nelson, only the second coach in the history of the team, resigned after a decade to become part-owner of the Golden State Warriors. Del Harris, Nelson's assistant and a former head coach of the Houston Rockets, took over the team. The Nelson era was over in Milwaukee.

Milwaukee's sixth man, Ricky Pierce.

THE WINNING STREAK COMES TO AN END

Del Harris began his stint as head coach with a team that played solid basketball but was still not aggressive enough to lead its division. In an effort to energize the team, Harris traded with the San Antonio Spurs for defensive specialist Alvin Robertson, whose quick hands helped him set new club records for steals. On offense, Ricky Pierce continued to provide outside firepower off the bench and was named the league's best sixth man. Still, the Bucks slipped to third place in the Central Division behind the more powerful Detroit Pistons and Chicago Bulls, each of which won NBA championships in the period between 1987 and 1991. The Bucks' playoff record did not improve either, as Milwaukee disappointed its fans by falling in the first round to Atlanta in 1987–88, in the second round to Detroit in 1988–89, in the first round to Chicago in 1989–90, and in the first round to Philadelphia in 1990–91.

Then, starting in 1991–92, Milwaukee dropped all the way out of the playoff picture. After 12 straight winning seasons, the Bucks had lost their edge. The team slid below .500 and fell toward the bottom of the NBA standings.

When the season opened the following year, a whole new team greeted Bucks fans. There was even a new coach, former Bucks player and assistant coach Mike Dunleavy. Dunleavy began rebuilding around an outstanding pair of rookies from the University of Arkansas, Lee Mayberry and Todd Day. They were known affectionately as "May-Day," the universal distress call. Sometimes that nickname seemed appropriate, for the team often seemed in trouble despite

Jack Sikma became the first Buck since 1978 to grab more than 10 rebounds per game.

All-Star forward Vin Baker (pages 26–27).

25

"May-Day's" best efforts. The young and inexperienced Bucks committed lots of turnovers and, unlike the Bucks teams under Don Nelson and Del Harris, had problems on defense. The result was a 28–54 record and seventh place in the Central Division.

The Bucks' woes continued over the next two seasons, but there was a silver lining to the gray clouds hanging over Milwaukee basketball fans. The low finishes meant high draft picks for the Bucks, and those translated into two terrifically talented players joining the club, Vin Baker and Glenn "Big Dog" Robinson.

1 9 9 3

Milwaukee won 10 of its first 13 games under new coach Mike Dunleavy.

First-round draft pick Lee Mayberry.

At first glance, Vin Baker and Glenn Robinson didn't have much in common. When Baker was selected in the first round in the 1993 college draft by Milwaukee, he was a relatively unknown player from the small University of Hartford. On the other hand, Robinson, who arrived the next year, was the NCAA Player of the Year and first pick overall, out of Big 10 powerhouse Purdue. Their styles of play were also very different. Powerful, 6-foot-11 Baker loved to pound inside for baskets and rebounds. Robinson, shorter at 6-foot-7 and less aggressive, preferred to shoot from the perimeter or to post his man up for shots inside.

Sherman Douglas made the team's only triple-double of the season (15 points, 11 assists, 10 rebounds).

Despite these differences, both players became successful quickly in the league. Baker was on the NBA All-Rookie team in 1993–94 and was named to the Eastern Conference All-Star squad each of the next three seasons. Robinson, under intense pressure because of his college honors, took a little longer to become a league star, but he consistently put up solid scoring and rebounding numbers. He was named to Dream Team III, the U.S. Olympic team in 1996, but had to miss the Olympics because of a foot injury.

For Milwaukee fans, Vin Baker and Glenn Robinson represented the best Bucks duo since Kareem Abdul-Jabbar and Oscar Robertson. During their first three years together in Milwaukee, Vin and Glenn each averaged more than 20 points per game and accounted for more than 40 percent of the Bucks' scoring and rebounding.

"Baker and Robinson are two of the brightest young stars in the game," said Milwaukee coach Chris Ford, who joined

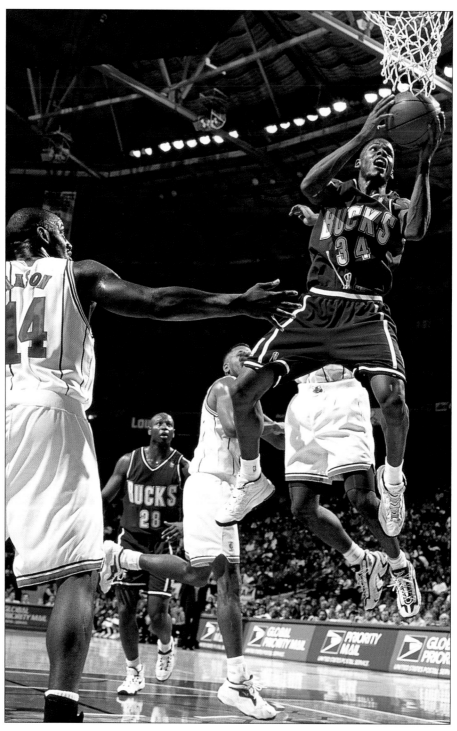

Young shooting guard Ray Allen.

"The Big Dog," Glenn Robinson.

1 9 9 7

Chucky Brown scored a season-high 13 points in a 132–123 win over New Jersey.

the team at the start of the 1996–97 season. "They're our go-to guys, the players we expect to lead us among the best teams in the NBA. The best news for us is that Vin and Glenn are only going to get better as players with each season and as we surround them with other talented people."

One of those talented people arrived via the college draft in 1996: shooting guard Ray Allen. The Bucks had actually drafted point guard Stephon Marbury, but swapped their pick with the Minnesota Timberwolves to acquire Allen and center Andrew Lang. "I'm glad it happened the way it did," said Allen. "Milwaukee is a good fit for me."

Allen also fit in right away with his new team. He became an instant starter and an instant sparkplug on offense. "Ray has excellent three-point range. He also moves well without the basketball and can shoot the ball coming off picks," remarked coach Ford. "He has a bright future here."

With Baker, Robinson, and Allen around, Milwaukee fans can believe their team's future prospects are also bright. Are the new Bucks equal in style and ability to Oscar Robertson, Kareem Abdul-Jabbar, Bob Dandridge, and Sidney Moncrief? That's a question that will be answered over time. One thing is for certain: these new Bucks intend to uphold a proud tradition of basketball excellence in Milwaukee. Bucks fans wouldn't expect anything else.